Larry's GREAT WESTERN

TEXT BY BILL DEAYTON-GROOM

WOLVERHAMPTON WANDERER 1

DAVID & CHARLES
Newton Abbot London North Pomfret (Vt)

THE TRAIN STANDING AT PLATFORM SEVEN IS THE ALREADY OVERCROWDED TRAIN FROM BIRKENHEAD GOING FORWARD TO LEAMINGTON SP BANBURY AND PADDINGTON — THE GWR APOLOGIS TO ALL THOSE PASSENGERS GETTING TRAMPLED O AND MAIMED IN THE CRUSH TO GET ON — AN AMBULANCE CAR WITH A FULL TEAM OF NURS IS PROVIDED AT THE REAR OF THE TRAIN.

British Library cataloguing in publication data

Larry
    Larry's Great Western
    1. English wit and humour, pictorial   2. Railroads —
    Caricatures
    Rn; Terence Parkes I. Title   II. Deayton-Groom, C. W.
    741.5′942   NC1476
    ISBN 0-7153-9069-4

Photoset in Linotron Joanna
by Northern Phototypesetting Co Bolton
and printed in Great Britain
by Butler & Tanner Limited Frome and London
for David & Charles Publishers plc
Brunel House   Newton Abbot   Devon

Published in the United States of America
by David & Charles Inc
North Pomfret   Vermont 05053   USA

The great Great Western Railway

Admirers of the Great Western are an on-going thing. Those who actually *knew* it become, inevitably, ever less. Yet there is never a shortage of enthusiastic recruits from the ranks of those who were, perhaps, not even born when the grey hand of nationalisation consigned it to a deliberately engineered historical dustbin.

But never to oblivion. It just won't lie down.

Many have been the learned pens which have attempted to explain the charisma which surrounded, still surrounds, that splendid Company. It certainly beats us. Perhaps it is because it was so right in almost everything it did. Perhaps it is beyond definition.

It was God's Wonderful Railway indeed!

Not the least aspect was its sheer *pleasantness* for, like all truly great people, the old GW had the broad-gauge capacity to laugh at itself. The following pages are dedicated, with affection, to this last of its many attributes.

Acknowledgement
Dimly remembered lines from the writer's extreme youth have been the inspiration for some of the verses. Those of obvious derivation and those which are probably 'anon' are offered equal appreciation.

LEARNER DRIVERS

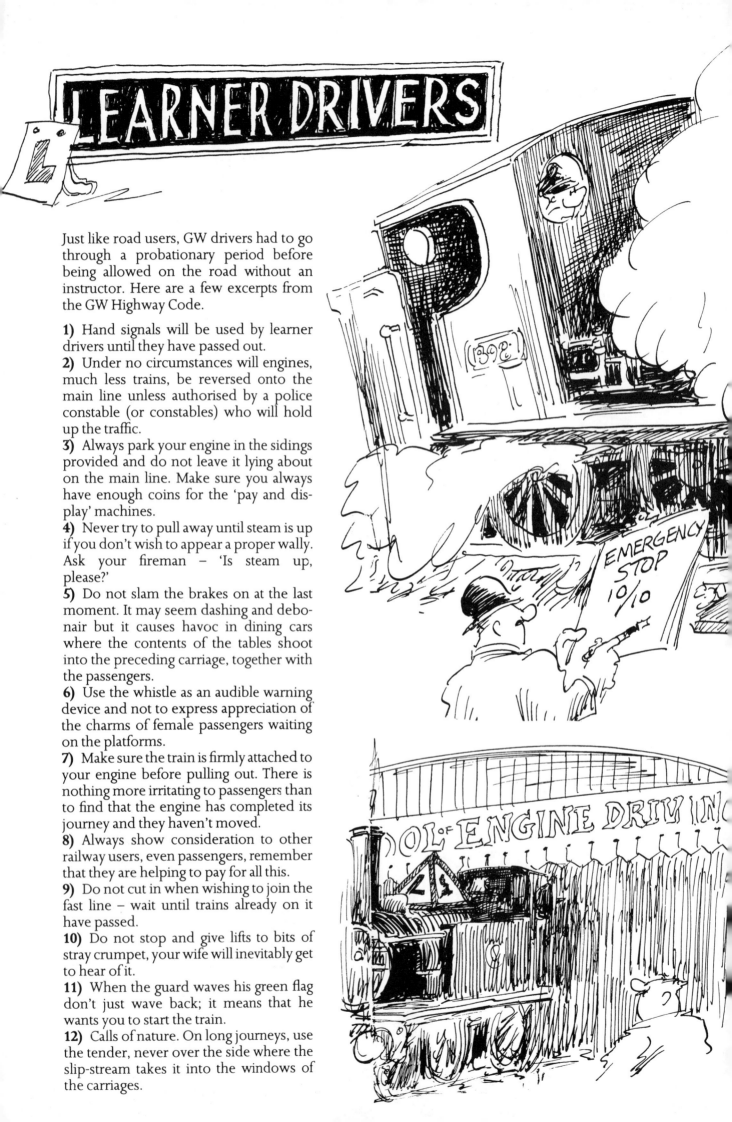

Just like road users, GW drivers had to go through a probationary period before being allowed on the road without an instructor. Here are a few excerpts from the GW Highway Code.

1) Hand signals will be used by learner drivers until they have passed out.

2) Under no circumstances will engines, much less trains, be reversed onto the main line unless authorised by a police constable (or constables) who will hold up the traffic.

3) Always park your engine in the sidings provided and do not leave it lying about on the main line. Make sure you always have enough coins for the 'pay and display' machines.

4) Never try to pull away until steam is up if you don't wish to appear a proper wally. Ask your fireman – 'Is steam up, please?'

5) Do not slam the brakes on at the last moment. It may seem dashing and debonair but it causes havoc in dining cars where the contents of the tables shoot into the preceding carriage, together with the passengers.

6) Use the whistle as an audible warning device and not to express appreciation of the charms of female passengers waiting on the platforms.

7) Make sure the train is firmly attached to your engine before pulling out. There is nothing more irritating to passengers than to find that the engine has completed its journey and they haven't moved.

8) Always show consideration to other railway users, even passengers, remember that they are helping to pay for all this.

9) Do not cut in when wishing to join the fast line – wait until trains already on it have passed.

10) Do not stop and give lifts to bits of stray crumpet, your wife will inevitably get to hear of it.

11) When the guard waves his green flag don't just wave back; it means that he wants you to start the train.

12) Calls of nature. On long journeys, use the tender, never over the side where the slip-stream takes it into the windows of the carriages.

A Fifty-Three-and-a-half Miles Idyll

At last I've got you on a slow train to Didcot
    All by ourselves alone,
Boy! how I'll pet you on this often stopping train
    And taste the blisses of non-stop kisses
Through this wonderful terrain.

As we go threading, our way through to Reading
    Entranced by the changing view,
Of Acton and Ealing, O Slough! how we are feeling
    Bewitched by the sight of you!

Twix't Pangbourne and Streatley, dearest how sweetly
    We pre-empt our honeymoon,
We're not finding Goring the slightest bit boring!
    But dam' Didcot's ten miles too soon.

'Though us drivers were always in charge of the engine,
    The guard was in charge of the train,
The guards, they were issued with Company watches,
    But not us – makes you wonder what brain
Decided a timepiece a bloomin' essential
    For a man who did not bear the brunt
Of keeping the timetable up to the mark,
    That was us – way up at the front!'

Firemen (1946–47)

'There's more, said the fireman, "to firin" an engine
   Than shovelin' coal through an 'ole,
If you don't get it right you get more smoke than steam
   And drivers (though nice on the whole)
Will give you the sharpest cut of their tongues
   If you don't get it under control.
What they put in the tenders in nineteen four six
   (Brought in from the United States)
Wouldn't burn down in Hades, no matter 'ow 'ot,
And much less in Great Western grates.
So if, in them days, your train sometimes was late,
   The journey a tedious crawl,
Remember us firemen was doin' our best –
   You were lucky to get there at all.'

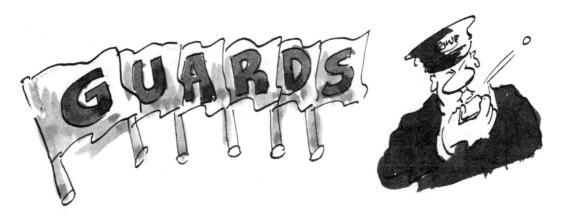

The General Manager,
Paddington.

Sir,
I was watching some of your chaps the other day and how they have the damn' cheek to call themselves Guards is beyond my comprehension. You want a completely new flag and whistle drill for a start. Send a batch of 'em down to us at Caterham and you'd soon see a difference!

I am *etc etc*
Rodney Fortinbrass Lt Col
Grenadier Guards.

WHO are these with anxious faces
    seen in towns and busy places
staggering under bags and cases?
    These, let me inform you sirs,
are Western Region passengers.
    Their immediate purpose is quite plain,
to buy a ticket, catch a train
    to their various destinations
from equally various railway stations.
    The ordeal they now face embraces
finding help with bags and cases,
    wives and aunts and sons and daughters
so they look around for porters
    who, tho' they are not deaf at all,
cannot hear them when they call
    but mutter through curled and callous lip
'The more the load, the less the tip.'
    refuse to heed the frantic flap
and go on playing ha-penny nap . . .

. . . When their final journey's ended
    will they find themselves suspended
in some ghost train 'twixt here and hell
    with wives and bags and kids as well?

No! their life on earth was tough,
    they have suffered quite enough . . .

. . . They shall have a Special Train
    stacked with limitless champagne,
served to them by topless birds
    with charming smiles and honeyed words,
driven by an angel with a lyre
    and cherubins to stoke the fire,
while houris wait in scented quarters –
    – and last of all ten thousand porters
(sent by forcible persuasion
    straight from hell for the occasion),
stuffed into trucks designed for cattle
    on springless wheels which jolt and rattle
with feet that hurt and ashen faces,
    carrying their bags and cases.

GANGERS

I WOULDN'T LEAVE MY LITTLE WOODEN HUT FOR YOU- OO ♫ ♪

STAFF NOTICE

(Immediate Action by Gangers)

Heavy smoking of Black Shag by Plate Laying Staff whilst on duty is causing the introduction of unnecessary fog services, the prevailing south-west winds carry the fog all over the System causing serious dislocation to the timetables. There have been cases of trains stuck as far back as Paddington, unable to move.

Gangers will ensure that smoking on the line will be only those brands of tobacco which have been cleared by the General Manager.

SAGA OF A WHEEL TAPPER (ex GWR)

Ham-fisted Harry was heavy on muscle
    But regretfully short on brain,
His job was lightly to tap all the wheels
    On each passing GW train.
(A melodious 'ting' meant all was OK,
    And, if not, a flat kind of 'dong')
Well within scope of the average IQ
    Even Harry could not go far wrong?

But Ham-fisted Harry wielded his hammer
    With might more than metal could stand,
And axle box, tyre, brake block and spring
    Just shattered to bits in his hand.
A new job for Harry had to be found,
    The accent a lot less on brains,
His vocation now? Cramming the public
    Into London's Underground trains.

TRAFFIC MANAGERS

ANNUAL DINNERS

Traffic Managers, like everyone else, have to eat and, in the 'great days' of the railways, their Annual Dinner was an event remarked upon for its style and impeccable good taste – even during an era when those desirable qualities were far more in day to day evidence than they are now. It was common knowledge that half the crowned heads of Europe unashamedly angled for invites, the Crown Prince of Monte Negro even offering to play the spoons in the cabaret in return for a ticket.

The Great Western was very much in evidence on the top table as befitted the largest system in terms of traffic before grouping; no single system possessing enough traffic managers to warrant hiring a coffee stall much less something like the Great Room at the Grosvenor, it was necessary to make the affair an all-companies thrash and, as there were some 120 railway companies in Britain in those far-off days, it was not difficult to make up a decent party.

Much leg-pulling was probably generated by members arriving late or not at all due to traffic problems on their systems but it is unlikely the bawling out ever got as bad as the House of Commons on one of their good days.

How the traffic actually managed whilst all this was going on is not recorded.

COMPLAINTS

Traffic Manager, Western Region, B.R.

Dear Sir,

I have been out of the Country for a bit, supervising the break-up of the Empire.

On my return last month I made my way to Paddington with the object of visiting a valued and loaded aunt who lives in the innermost recesses of the West Country, confident that a half dozen changes would bring me and a considerable pile of luggage to her local Station as of yore.

I was advised that the half-dozen changes had been taken off by a man called Beeching and that the resultant gaps are now filled by local transport.

The 'local transport' turned out to be bus services which run only on market days, weather permitting.

I arrived at my aunt's a day late by means of hired cars, the rapacity of the drivers of which can be equalled only by that of the politicians of the newly independent countries I have worked so hard to set up.

Punctuality is a fetish of my aunt and I therefore stand a good chance of losing my inheritance.

This would never have happened in Great Western days. Can I sue this Beeching?

Yours etc.

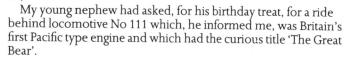

To the Traffic Manager. 9th May 1924

Sir,

My young nephew had asked, for his birthday treat, for a ride behind locomotive No 111 which, he informed me, was Britain's first Pacific type engine and which had the curious title 'The Great Bear'.

I accordingly telephoned Paddington and asked when No 111 would next be on duty. They were most helpful and gave me a train which stops at Reading and which would allow me to get the boy home in good time.

I duly purchased two first-class tickets and having passed the barrier (an ordeal in itself) we progressed to the front of the train to admire the engine.

Although No 111, the engine was not 'Great Bear' at all but one bearing the inscription 'Viscount Churchill' (who he?). The driver told us that it had been the 'Great Bear' but had been cut down to 'Castle Class' size by having two of its wheels removed.

The whole upshot was that my nephew's birthday treat had been loused up and I had to take him to Fortnums for a slap-up tea by way of compensation.

Lopping off wheels and changing names in this feckless manner is misleading to the public and savours of getting revenue by false pretences. I suggest the least that you can do is to refund the fare and settle Fortnum's bill which I enclose.

Yours indignantly,

To the General Manager   17th July 1938
Paddington.

Dear Sir,

    Whenever I arrive at Paddington and pass the engine on my way to the barrier I always experience a twinge of envy – how do you keep them so clean and beautiful? Could you tell me where you recruit your domestics? Alternatively, could I send Ivy to you for a course?

    Yours faithfully,
      Cynthia Margaret Hall (Mrs)
Cheltenham.

CARRIAGE CLEANING

CLEANERS

The Iron Horse was a noble beast but, it must be admitted, it was also a dirty one, consequently armies of cleaners needed to be employed to remove the grime from the rolling stock.

Various means were used to ease the task and increase the efficiency of the cleaners. On the GW during the early 20s a steam driven vacuum cleaner was used with some success. Its miniature boiler was fired by a spirit lamp, a two cylinder engine with Stephensons link motion created the vacuum and turned the brushes; by linking up the reverser the machine would automatically empty itself straight into the dustbin.

The concept had eventually to be abandoned as the equipment could never be left unattended without the fuel tank being rifled by layabouts after the meths.

GREAT WESTERN MARSHALLING YARD SCANDAL

The Foreman dwelt in his semi-detached
    And so did his daughter Lilo,
Forsooth she was a nubile wench
    With a fol-de-rol-de-ride-O

Full many a shunter came to woo
    And all lecherous they sighed-O
For the Foreman took size twelve in boots
    With a fol-de-rol-de-ride-O

But a shunter called Bert called at dead o'night
    And shunted her into his hide-O
Then switched himself onto the up main line
    With a fol-de-rol-de-ride-O

The Foreman still dwells in his semi-detached
    But not with his daughter Lilo,
For the maid has found a more lucrative trade
    With a fol-de-rol-de-ride-O

GWR/LMS RIVALRY

There was healthy rivalry between all the old railway companies and that between the GW and the London & North Western (later part of the LMS) was particularly intense. There are many who say (with some truth) that the LNWR never had a decent locomotive after the demise of Ramsbottom until the line became part of the LMS and then not until William Stanier went to Crewe from Swindon.

Here is some correspondence which may faintly reflect the situation in those early days.

The Chairman,
The Great Western Railway,
Paddington.   7th October 1903

Deer Sir,
   My enemy in the Third, Webb Miner, says that Mr Churchward's tapered boilers are threw some rotten plate rolling at Swindon. I tell him that they was desined like that but he is potty on the L.N.W.R. (because his name is the same as Mr F. Webb and his rotten compounds) and he won't beleeve me. Please tell me how I can anser this rotter and put him in his rotten plaice.
   Yrs. Faithfully,

Master Thomas Merry
St James School,
Sussex.   21st October 1903

My dear Merry,
   Yes, our boilers do indeed taper. I must say I was a bit surprised and referred your letter to Swindon for explanation. Mr Churchward went on to some length, most of which I confess I did not understand, but it seems that our boilers produce steam which is hot, dry and in large quantities which is how the engine likes it and at lower cost which is how we like it. Mr Churchward's remarks about Mr Webb do not bear repeating to young ears.
   I trust there is enough here for you to put that little creep Webb minor in his place.
   Perhaps you could help me – what are the 'compounds' to which you made reference?
   Yours sincerely,

MEALS on WHEELS

IN very early days four wheels was the normal for rolling stock, experiment had found that anything less caused repeated and irritating derailment.

First-class passengers, trying to get a bite in the style to which they were accustomed, surely found the miniscule compartments restrictive for even a simple meal like luncheon. How did they cope with ten courses together with appropriate wines without servants? Or did they have a manservant or two with them? If so, where did they put them? Obviously not squeezed in with the quality, perhaps they were stationed on the running boards, one each side, handing the plates through the windows. The resulting detritus of game pie, steak, kidney, mushroom and oyster pudding, trout bones, straw and grit clogging the floor and getting into the ladies' shoes must have made the second-class with their genteel sandwiches and coffee seem positively clinical. The third-class, with no top cover at all and precious little at the sides, probably never risked anything more friable than faggots or black pudding.

Great Western passengers were in better case, the broad gauge allowing a picnic style meal to be enjoyed without the diners putting their elbows into each others mouths. Strangely, the GW had no restaurant car stock until standard-gauge days which seems a pity – what an opportunity for displays of dignified Victorian opulence was lost!

Unable to expand sideways, the railways were forced to go lengthways and wheels multiplied from four to six, eight and finally an immoderate twelve. Restaurant and kitchen cars appeared and in the galleys huge black stoves with glowing fires could turn out anything from a baron of beef to a custard tart. Wine was carried in variety but not in cellars which would have got in the way of the wheels.

On the GW, of course, everything was driven by steam including the clocks for timing the minute steaks.

INSTRUCTIONS TO STAFF

1) Royal personages will be treated with utmost respect short of actually grovelling. Staff must bear in mind the dignity of the Company.

2) Station Masters will wear Company best issue frock-coat and top hat and ensure they are brushed and free from gravy stains, fag ash and so on.

3) Staff will not hang around Royal travellers hoping for a tip.

4) Ticket Collectors will not demand to see Royal tickets at barriers. The Directors will already have checked on this.

5) Carriage staff will ensure Royal lavatories are furnished with No 1 issue Company paper with GW Coats of Arms embossed.

6) Staff will not address Royal personages unless spoken to first. This rule may be waived in the event of a grave emergency, viz:-

a) Royal lady's crinoline on fire.
b) Royal personage standing in path of oncoming express.
c) HRH Prince of Wales lighting up cigar in non-smoker.

7) Train stewards will keep thumbs out of Royal dishes, particularly soup. The practice of polishing off smear on Royal spoon with pocket handkerchief will cease.

8) Engine drivers are reminded that manning a Royal Train is an honour in itself and are not to expect an M.V.O. or other marks of Royal approval.

9) Firemen will ensure coal in tender is best Welsh and polished.

10) The Directors reserve sole rights for any tokens of Royal esteem that may be flying about and forbid all attempts by staff to horn in.

THE custom of wearing a leek in honour of St David on 1 March is said to originate from a recognition symbol in a battle against the Saxons, although certain historians say that the plant chosen by the Saint was really a daffodil. How, then, did the pot herb get in? Some schools of thought maintain that the leek was introduced by Hywel the Indifferent who deemed that a national symbol which could also be eaten would serve a dual purpose in times of national crisis.

The GW did good business sending train loads of leeks into S. Wales from the market gardens of Old England and a similar operation was performed for N. Wales by the LNWR (later LMS). When Welsh Wizard David Lloyd George reintroduced the daffodil, horticulturalists in Lincolnshire swiftly hopped onto the gravy train and another rich vein of revenue was released.

The inhabitants of the Principality now had a choice as to what they could stuff into their lapels on 1 March (if they wished to get from one end of the High Street to the other without being assaulted for suspected English sympathies).

FAMOUS LAST WORDS
CAPITALS UNITED EXPRESS
063
MAVIS—YOU'LL HAVE TO GET OUT AND PUSH

BROAD GAUGE

Damsels in Distress

Writers of Victorian melodrama tended to avoid placing their action in Great Western territory as the broad gauge inhibited them using one of their favourite heart-stoppers – tying the heroine to the rail in the path of the next express. Seven feet tall actresses did not come to hand easily and scarcity enabled them to name their own price.

There are other implications. Could the average villain have coped with a 7ft heroine? Would the average villain (cowards at heart) have risked being overpowered by the giantess and find himself tied to the rail? Could the average hero be relied upon to turn up and effect a rescue (7ft heroines are not everyone's cup of tea)?

And what, in heaven's name, could be a villain's motives in tying a girl to the line in the first place (assuming she was of standard gauge height)? If he had tired of her surely there were neater solutions to cooling affections? If *she* had rejected *him* in favour, say, of the hero there are better and less final means of coercion than the flanges of a railway wheel.

Then there is the practical side of the business. Supposing the train was late, or even cancelled? There is the villain kicking his heels and feeling more a wally every moment. The last straw is when he has to release the girl because she is 'dying to spend a penny' and by the time she has finished the train has come and gone and there's not another until 8.30 tomorrow morning. Any decent villain would turn on his heel in disgust.

War Office Memo to GWR — 17th January 1917

The enemy is making ever increasing use of the aeroplane on (or over) the Western Front and is now extending this form of operation over the United Kingdom itself. It need hardly be stressed how important the railway systems are in the successful prosecution of this war.

Last month a train on the London, Brighton & South Coast Railway carrying a vital consignment of Sam Browne Belts (Officers for the use of) was shot up on its way to France by von Richtofen's Flying Circus.

Suitable camouflage can make a train almost invisible from the air. A light framework carrying strips of suitably coloured rags has been used with success for important installations in the battle areas. We enclose drawings which show how the system can be adapted for railway use together with sample colours for the rags.

King and Country expect your full co-operation.

I have the honour to be etc. etc.

Memo from GWR to War Office — 1st March 1917

Reference yours of 17th January on Train Camouflage. Our Swindon Works fitted out a train in the manner set out in your drawings.

Between Slough and Reading sparks from the chimney set fire to the coloured rags and the whole train was burnt out. Fifty-three wagons were packed to their roofs with Sam Browne Belts en route to Yeovil for urgent refurbishment. All were a total loss.

Quite apart from the loss of vital military equipment, our Company sustained a badly damaged 'Bulldog' class mixed traffic engine and the total loss of fifty-three wagons and a brake van. Not to mention a valued driver, fireman and guard who are still in a state of shock.

Our assessors are still working out the cost which will, of course, be down to the War Office and their bum steer.

King and Country are entitled to expect better than this.

We have the honour to be etc. etc.

RAILWAY HOUSES

The rectory or vicarage is usually influenced by ecclesiastic architecture – pointed windows and doors, stone mullions, an odour of sanctity and dry rot, the whole often festooned in a throttling mantle of ivy.

Railway homes are similarly influenced by the main stream – fretwork gables, windows which are raised and lowered by a strap, a 12″ gap between the end of the path and the series of nearly verticle steps to the front door and rooms lined with antimaccassar infested plush benches. The kitchen is reminiscent in size and shape of the dining-car galley, right down to the rattle of pots, pans and cutlery everytime a train thunders along the embankment some ten feet away. Some of the larger houses have a semaphore signalling system indicating when the loo is free or engaged.

WRECKHAM HALL

DO NOT USE THE PRIVVY WHILE A TRAIN IS IN THE VICINITY

Fill the steins for old lang syne
    Don't shout or we'll be chucked out,
Stand (if you can) and drink a toast once again
    With pints of Guinesses Park Royal Stout!
Think of all those happy hours
    Spent waiting for the train,
And drink to all who may be absent,
    Who've missed the bloomin' train again!

July 1938

BIRTHS

To Shunter Sidney Globes and his wife Bertha a son, Kevin. The infant Globes had a birth weight of no less than 29 lbs 12ozs, surely a GW record! Delivery was by Caesarean Section.

To Sir Frederick Grate-Import, Bart. and Lady Grate-Import a daughter. We are delighted to report this popular Director's good news. The bonny infant weighed 6 lbs 1½ozs at birth, surely a GW record! Names chosen for the little beauty are Elizabeth, Mary, Alexandra, Victoria, Adelaide, Edna; the first five to honour our Royal Family and the last after her elegant and talented mother. Said Sir Frederick, 'I've already got him down for Eton, the Turf Club, Marylebone C.C., the London Welsh, Whites, Bootles and the Irish Guards. No doubt I will come up with a few more!' Congratulations, Sir Frederick!

To Trundle, Albert, Porter at Acton Station & Mrs Trundle, a son.

To Head of Complaints Department, Paddington, Claude (Grouser) Gripe and Mrs Gripe, septuplets. Observed 'Grouser', 'No bother for once in my life, it was like shelling peas!' Commented Mona, (Mrs Gripe) to our reporter, 'We've only been married three months; from now on he sleeps at the local, he spends most of his time there anyway.'

To Clipper, Walter, Ticket Clerk at Slough & Mrs Clipper, a daughter. We are not often moved to levity but – Good luck to the Nipper, Clipper!

GWR Staff Magazine, July 1938

GW ROMANCE

Wales and the West of England have had strong romantic associations since King Arthur, the Round Table and the ladies of the court whose relations seemed in a constant state of flux suggesting that bed would have been a more fitting symbol for the brotherhood than a table. And did not Young Lochinvar come out of the west, or was that Scotland? And what about Lorna Doone and Girt Jan Ridd? But of course all these goings and comings would have been on horseback and long before the days of the GWR.

Probably one of the most romantic romances of more modern times in which the GW played an important part was that of the Honourable Barbara Frippett, her lover Sir John Manley-Cocks and her betrothed the Earl of Smallhampton. This is what happened.

In the summer of 1886 the Honourable Barbara, a noted beauty, was induced against her will to become engaged to the Earl of Smallhampton by her formidable father Viscount Frippett of Maidenhead, a fanatical fly-fisherman. Through Smallhampton's estates ran five miles of the best trout fishing in the country and the Viscount was avid to get his hands or, to be more accurate, his flies on it. Hence the enforced betrothal.

The Viscount was aware of Sir John's ambitions regarding his daughter and the lady was constantly watched, making communication between the lovers well nigh impossible. Sir John was a resourceful young man and managed to acquire some thousands of feet of the overhead railway found in every haberdashery establishment of the day for transporting money from the counter to the cash desk. By working mostly at night he fixed a somewhat tortuous line over the rooftops from his flat in Jermyn Street to his lady's bedroom window in the family's town house in St. James Street.

Contact thus established, Sir John was able to learn that the Viscount with the Viscountess and his daughter would be travelling from Paddington to the family seat near Maidenhead on a certain day together with the time of the train. At the cost of a £5 note Sir John borrowed a carriage key from a carriage cleaner and, having seen the family safely into their compartment, promptly locked the door. The Hon Barbara then excused herself to 'adjust her toilette' and Sir John locked the door on the corridor side. He then removed the lady from the train just as it was about to pull out.

They were married that same morning in the church of a small village near Kenilworth the living of which happened to be in Sir John's gift. The irony of the story is that the Earl, on hearing the news, died from a stroke having recently made a will in favour of his betrothed so that the now Lady Manley-Cocks inherited the Smallhampton estates, they not being entailed. She let her father fish there once a year on his birthday.

WEDDINGS

The bells are ringing for me and my girl
  The drunks are singing for me and my girl
And the hair of my Hetty
  Is choked with confetti
The compartment is knee-deep in rice.

Her mother's weeping for me and my girl
  Her father's keeping for me and my girl
The cost of the liquor
  The fee of the vicar
But is free with unwanted advice.

They're celebrating for me and my girl
  The train is waiting for me and my girl
On the rack are our cases
  We are both in our places
As the window slides past the last guest.

The slip's slip-streaming for me and my girl
  The engine's steaming for me and my girl
Fast, fast goes the blast
  But it can't blast too fast
To our honeymoon home in the west.

THE G.W.R APOLOGISES —
FOR THE LATE RUNNING
OF THE 12:30 WEDDING
— THE APPROXIIMATF TIME
OF THE BRIDE'S ARRIVAL
WILL NOW BE 1-15 PM

We are pleased to report that Cedric Carbon of Old Oak Common has stepped up the ladder of promotion from Under Assistant Deputy Fireman (Temporary) to Under Assistant Deputy Fireman. Interviewed, Carbon commented modestly 'And I've only been with the Company eleven years! Now me and Bev can get spliced at last.' Added Beverly Cake, Cedric's intended, 'I feel quite dizzy! Where will it all end?'

Announcing his forthcoming wedding, Nigel Bitumen told us 'Now I've moved up from Porter/Signalman to Signal/Porter I shall have enough for two!' Bitumen will install his bride in one of the Company's newly built cottages. 'Nigel says that our new home has an inside toilet,' bubbled Marlene Pelmet, his intended bride, with understandable excitement, 'I shall feel like a film star!'

Extract from GWR Staff Magazine, June 1923

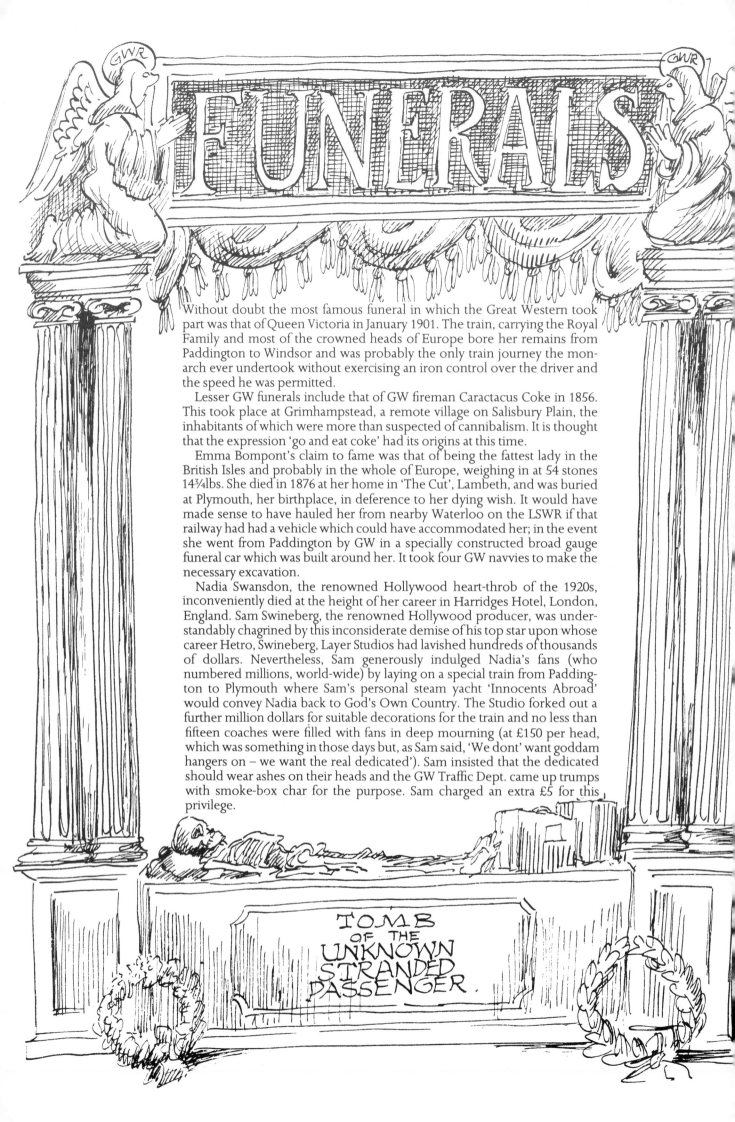

FUNERALS

Without doubt the most famous funeral in which the Great Western took part was that of Queen Victoria in January 1901. The train, carrying the Royal Family and most of the crowned heads of Europe bore her remains from Paddington to Windsor and was probably the only train journey the monarch ever undertook without exercising an iron control over the driver and the speed he was permitted.

Lesser GW funerals include that of GW fireman Caractacus Coke in 1856. This took place at Grimhampstead, a remote village on Salisbury Plain, the inhabitants of which were more than suspected of cannibalism. It is thought that the expression 'go and eat coke' had its origins at this time.

Emma Bompont's claim to fame was that of being the fattest lady in the British Isles and probably in the whole of Europe, weighing in at 54 stones 14¾lbs. She died in 1876 at her home in 'The Cut', Lambeth, and was buried at Plymouth, her birthplace, in deference to her dying wish. It would have made sense to have hauled her from nearby Waterloo on the LSWR if that railway had had a vehicle which could have accommodated her; in the event she went from Paddington by GW in a specially constructed broad gauge funeral car which was built around her. It took four GW navvies to make the necessary excavation.

Nadia Swansdon, the renowned Hollywood heart-throb of the 1920s, inconveniently died at the height of her career in Harridges Hotel, London, England. Sam Swineberg, the renowned Hollywood producer, was understandably chagrined by this inconsiderate demise of his top star upon whose career Hetro, Swineberg, Layer Studios had lavished hundreds of thousands of dollars. Nevertheless, Sam generously indulged Nadia's fans (who numbered millions, world-wide) by laying on a special train from Paddington to Plymouth where Sam's personal steam yacht 'Innocents Abroad' would convey Nadia back to God's Own Country. The Studio forked out a further million dollars for suitable decorations for the train and no less than fifteen coaches were filled with fans in deep mourning (at £150 per head, which was something in those days but, as Sam said, 'We dont' want goddam hangers on – we want the real dedicated'). Sam insisted that the dedicated should wear ashes on their heads and the GW Traffic Dept. came up trumps with smoke-box char for the purpose. Sam charged an extra £5 for this privilege.

TOMB
OF THE
UNKNOWN
STRANDED
PASSENGER.

HOLIDAYS

Down to the sea, down to the sea!
   With bucket and spade and Billy and me
From Paddington Station
   With my fav'rite relation,
Down to the sea and winkles for tea.

Down to the sea, down to the sea!
   That is the way for Jenny and me
And my gym-slippered miss
   Has allowed me a kiss
But hurry or Mummy will see.

Down to the sea, down to the sea!
   Bobby sox'd, glamour-pants Mary and me
I'm becoming obsessed
   With her legs and her breast
But no higher my lad or I'll whop you says she.

Down to the sea, down to the sea!
   To a little hotel for Sally and me,
We intend to spend
   A dirty weekend
And we go to the bar for a large gin and T.

RACING PIGEONS AT PADDINGTON

Ron Bumstead, when not in the pub,
   was an active member of the Pigeon Club
near Goole whose members entered races
   by sending birds to distant places
by rail, hoping that their pigeon might
   prove to make the fastest flight.

Now, of all Ron's feathered host,
   Meg (Ron's missus) favoured most
a cock by name of Dan, for Meg
   had loved him since he was an egg
and urged Ron to give Dan a shot
   in the next race but Ron said 'What?
He's dim, his navigation's hazy
   the bugger is, moreover, lazy'.

But Dan went in the fixture list
   ('Alright Meg, if you insist')
And she, from loyalty to her pet,
   decided on a ten pound bet
with bookie, Honest Charlie Dodds
   at a 100 to 1 (Dan's 'no chance' odds).

Off went the pigeons for the race
   to Kings Cross, packed in wicker case,
then Paddington by parcels van,
   all eager – all excepting Dan.
An idle bird, Dan, but no goose
   he noticed that the lid was loose
and, ere the guard could raise a shout,
   he'd squirmed and wriggled his way out.

Up into the roof he fluttered,
    'Sod the bird' the train guard muttered
(referring to the truant flyer)
    and fixed the lid with copper wire
observing, when the task was ended,
    'The less that's said, the soonest mended'.

From his perch, with beady eye,
    Dan watched the basket loaded by
the guard into the train – to where?
    Dan didn't know and didn't care
but headed for Trafalgar Square
    where, he'd heard, with morals lax
the lady birds are found in stacks.

Each hen received Dan's close attention
    with practised prod in the right direction
each taking Dan ten seconds flat,
    with a finale on Lord Nelson's hat.
'Like him', mused Dan, 'I've done my duty,
    and now for Goole and home and beauty'.
and, by exerting all his powers,
    he made the trip in eighteen hours.

Squealed Meg, as she saw Dan alight,
    'It's Dan!' said Ron 'By gum you're right!
I've right misjudged that little cock.'
    and punched Dan's leg tag in the clock.

By homing via Trafalgar Square
    he'd made it with a day to spare;
as clocks can't lie Dan was *proved* quicker,
    so Meg picked up a thousand nicker.

To the Pigeon Fancy, in anticipation.
Poetic licence has been used by the poet whenever he felt like it.

CRIMINAL CLASS

Today, with crime threatening to become an Estate of the Realm, if one were asked to guess how many of one's fellow passengers were crooks one would be tempted to answer 'the lot' to be on the safe side. In Great Western days guessing which was the odd man out was far more difficult, nevertheless the game is still worth playing as a means of relieving the tedium of a long journey, or even a short one. Here are some tips which might be useful.

Well-bred people (apart from politicians) tend not to advertise their professions and that applies particularly to the underworld. It should be remembered that appearances can be misleading and the fellow with eyes an inch apart and reading a copy of the Khama Sutra could be a bishop in mufti engaged in some urgent research work for the next synod; the girl with the cornflower blue eyes and the air of an upper-class angel might well be carrying a bicycle-chain in her reticule and the effulgence from the Cheryble brothers in the corner seats might well be covering a discussion on a take-over bid which will put 5,000 people out of work. You just can't tell.

But on the old Great Western one could be pretty sure that the gentleman in broad arrows handcuffed to the granite faced man in the blue uniform was on his way for a holiday on Dartmoor.

CUISINE

Famous bon viveur Egon Toast, with his wife Melba, spend a day on GW trains to see for themselves what fast food is like. Unfortunately the highest speed was reached after luncheon when they were asleep.

Well, there we were, in the Restaurant Car of our first train at 8.45am precisely. George, our steward, produced the menu and Melba was delighted to see that her favourite brand of cornflakes was on it. I started with the porridge (4d) and Melba, of course, cornflakes (2½d); the porridge was full-bodied and creamy with no lumps, the cornflakes were corny and flakey and up to Melba's exacting standards. For the main course I chose two fried eggs, sunny side up and four rashers of bacon (Danish back. 9d) with a slice of French bread as I like to sop up the fat (½d). Melba went for the sausages and chips (8d). My eggs were fresh and well fried and served up on a really hot plate but I could have done with a bit more hot fat. Melba's sausages were about 4ins long and about 1in thick. Melba ordered coffee (1½d) but I had tea as coffee tends to give me wind if I have it before 11.00am. We wound up with toast and marmalade (3d). A promising start to the day and all expertly served by George who thoroughly deserved his 3d tip.

Elevenses were taken in our reserved compartment. Melba had her usual mocha but I went for the good old Camp which is kinder to delicate tummies! We ordered a Mars Bar apiece as it would be nearly two hours to luncheon (5½d).

We changed trains for luncheon and introduced ourselves to Fred, our new steward. Fred arranged a superb table by the window for us and we were both charmed by the decor, particularly the sepia prints of Barnstaple in bygone days. I selected an avocado pear steeped in vodka for starters (1/–) and Melba had a pancake (3d), there is no doubt that vodka really peps up that rather flaccid fruit and is highly recommended, the pancake was all one would expect a pancake to be, round and flat. There were no less than four choices for main course and Fred recommended the lamb cutlets with mint jelly (1/2) with creamed potatoes (K. Edwards) and sprouts (Brussels) for vegetables (7½d). Melba had Shepherds Pie (8½d) with limitless HP Sauce to help it down (no charge). Next I chose apple pie and custard (7d) and

I THINK THAT CHAP ON THE EXETER TRAIN WANTS TO BORROW OUR SAUCE

Melba apple crumble (4d). The cutlets were tender and just a little bit crisp on the outside, but the creamed potatoes! King Edward would have been proud of them! The sprouts had been caught by the frost, excellent. I was unable to see much of Melba's Shepherds Pie because of the smothering of sauce; anyhow, she did not complain. We finished off with cheese, biscuits and coffee (5½d). For 9/6 (including a bottle of Wincarnis and tip) we had really been done proud and Fred produced a bottle of bismuth tablets at no charge!

As we were staying on the same train for tea we decided to retire to our compartment and 'bide a wee' whilst we settled our lunch. At 4 o'clock sharp the faithful Fred tapped on the door with tea on a silver tray (Assam) and biscuits (Huntley & Palmers Tea Time Assortment). As I watched Melba pouring I reflected how lucky we were to be English, what other countries have this charming custom of afternoon tea? And all for 7d!

We boarded yet another train for dinner and immediately sorted out our steward to see where he had put us – we need not have worried, a special table for two with a spray of flowers for my lady wife! Albert was the name of our new Maitre and the menu was well up to what we had come to expect. For soup we both chose Brown Windsor (a must on the Great Western) and very good it was, thick, glutinous and very, very brown (3½d). For fish I favoured the coley au gratin (5d) and Melba went for the fried rock salmon because there is no trouble with the bones, she finds that she can chew them up. (4d). Then I ordered jugged hare, pois (petit), asparagus tips in melted butter, saute potatoes and redcurrant jelly (2/6). Melba asked for roast Surrey chicken, turnips and butter beans (1/3). I had a second helping of the hare (no charge) but Melba asked to be excused her turnips. With the main course we had a carafe of the house red, very potable (3/–). Spotted Dick has always been a favourite pudding with me and I had some yellow chartreuse poured over it before Albert added the custard (9d), Melba had the trifle but without the sherry (3d). And then, of course, cheese, biscuits and coffee (7d all in).

We finished just as the train pulled into Paddington, just in time for us to visit a favourite restaurant for a light supper – but that's another story!

THE GREAT WESTERN BROTHERS at PADDERS

There's 'Booters' – Bootles and old 'Whiters' – Whites
And, of course, 'Athers' for literary types,
But for sheer exhilaration give us Paddington Station
And the Dining Room's nameless delights.
So play the game, cads,
    When you're dining at 'Padders'
And refrain from fraternal fights.
    At Padders' the cream of us lads
    Forgather to meet fellow cads –
An M P or, more sinister,
    A Cabinet Minister
Or perhaps, with his mistress, our dads.
    So play the game chaps,
        And turn a blind eye
    For all of us have our pet fads!
    (I say, what about bringing those
Southern sisters here for a spot
of Brown Windsor soup, Kenneth?
Don't rock the gravy boat, George.)

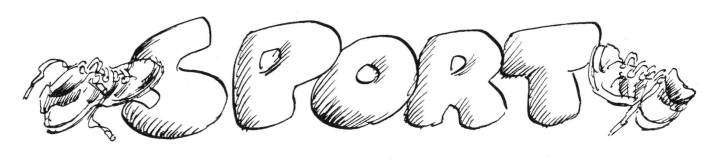

SPORT

In the best traditions of the 'Boy's Own Paper' GW staff were mad keen on sport as a means of maintaining physical fitness necessary to keep the service to the olympian standards set by the GW Board. Some staff were so dedicated to that end as to make valiant attempts to extend the principle into duty hours.

Golf was only moderately successful as most depots were short on fairways; level crossing gates offered possibilities for tennis but, generally speaking, athletics were a better proposition than ball games. The long-jump (across the tracks from one platform to the other), pole vaulting (over the footbridge), Shot-putting (with hand luggage), hurdling (over milk churns) and hop, step and jump along the sleepers were all highly popular.

Footplate and train staff were necessarily restricted until Gordon Westbury, a guard, broke through with water ski-ing along the pick-up troughs from a rope tied to the rear lamp bracket.

POLITICS

Great Western people were not overly involved with politics until 1946/7 brought the threat of nationalisation which they vigorously resisted, regretfully without success. Inevitably there was some passive involvement such as carrying Liberal MPs from Cornwall, Labour MPs from South Wales and Tory MPs from Cheltenham to and from Westminster and, probably on more than one occasion, Karl Marx together with wife, family and the housemaid he currently favoured for a West Country holiday as the guest of the long-suffering Engels.

More intriguing is that, from 1913 to 1946, Olga Krumpetovitch, a beautiful Russian, practically lived on the Great Western at the expense first of the Czar and, later, of the Soviet Government. Results were virtually nil as everyone knew she was a spy and, indeed, was positively favoured by MI5 lest she was replaced by someone more efficient. The ageing beauty was eventually liquidated by Molotov from whom she had tried to extract information about night life in the Kremlin.

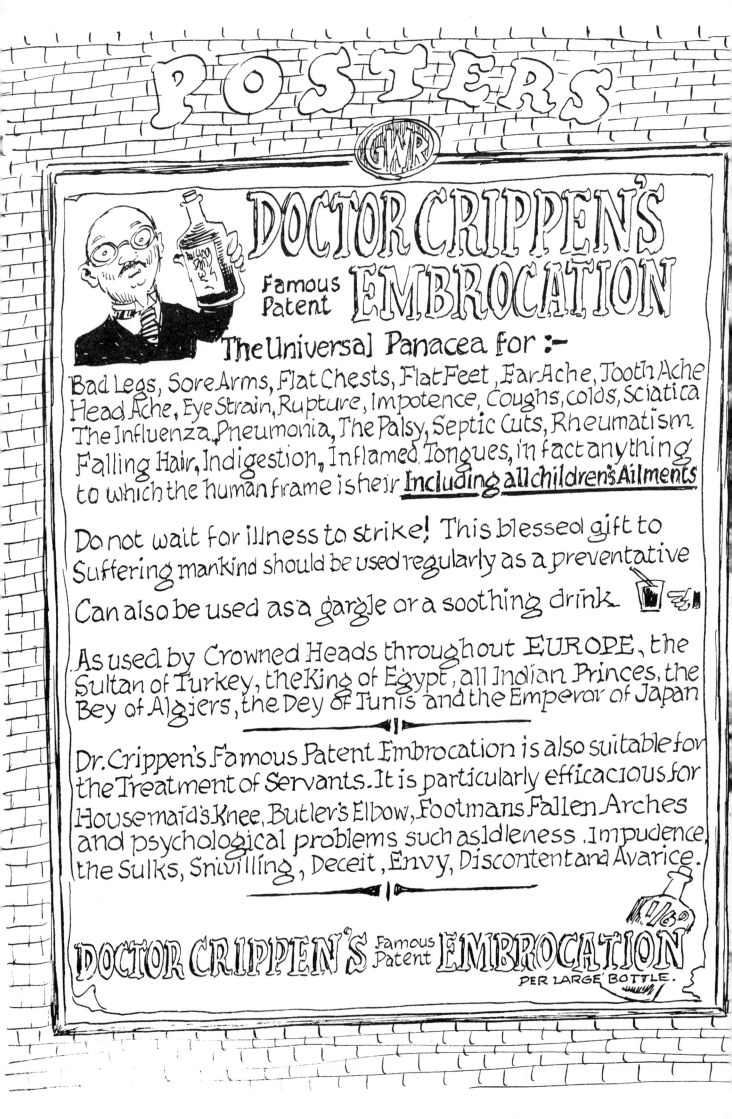

BOOK REVIEWS

Great Western Goods Trucks *by O. Spock*
(Barbara Allen   1/6)

The history of GW goods vehicles is traced from the early iron age through broad gauge days, when not enough traffic could be found to fill the cavernous wagons, to modern times when there are never enough GW wagons to fill the traffic. This curious situation is brought about by all systems retaining each other's stock against possible shortages of their own. The consequence is that the GW have more trucks owned by other companies on their metals than their own. Large users tried supplying their own 'private owners wagons' in desperate attempts to get their products moving. You can't miss them, they can be any colour except grey and the owners' names are writ large; they stand, immovably locked, in sidings throughout the Country.

Platform Machines on the GW *by The Rev. Cedric Chausable*
(Hamburger Press   1/3)

Ever tried getting a bar of Nestle's excellent chocolate from one of those red machines and found it jammed with penny-sized washers? The author gives invaluable tips on not only how to free the drawer but how to induce the machine to cough up the goods without further investment. The technique is also applicable to cigarette and weighing machines and platform tickets; we accompany Mr Chausable on an imaginary trip by stopping train from Paddington to Padstow with full details. Sadly, since the publication of this interesting little volume, Mr Chausable has been unfrocked.

Buffers on GW Goods Sidings *by Xavier Glue*
(MacGonnigle   3/–)

Someone once said 'of the making of railway books there is no end', or words to that effect – but Buffers! surely this is pushing it a bit? Nevertheless the writer has managed some 2,500 pages on the subject. Here's joy for the determined masochist.

Through Darkest Africa by Pannier Tank   *by Viscount Peckham of the Gorbals*
(Chas & Dave   2/6)

An expensive read but worth every penny. Lord Gorbals tells us how he travelled from the port of Ululati in Luxembourg West Africa to New Wigan in British East Equatorial Africa on a 0–6–0 Pannier Tank Engine which he picked up at the Swindon spring sales in 1929. This daunting feat was achieved with the help of the 9th battalion, the King's African Pioneer Corps (Prince Consort's Own). These splendid fellows laid the track ahead of the loco and took it up again when the engine had passed, coal and other supplies being carried in baskets on the heads of Basuto porters. Enthralling account of crossing the Zambesi with the track resting on inflated agouti skins.

The Compleat Fireman   *by Ted Damper (Fireman retd.)*
(McVite & Palmer   1/–)

For the armchair footplate man. The artists of the shovel possessed techniques which would turn a Wimbledon No 1 seed green with envy, Ace of Spades Fireman, Ed. Fibula, being reckoned to have the best back hand throw on the whole of the system, if not in the whole of the Country. Ted takes the wraps off many footplate mysteries such as operating a 10ft long poker, how to work an injector without being scalded to death, producing perfectly fried eggs on the shovel without burning the bacon and how to tell, at a glance, what they've put in the tender – from best Welsh steam to nutty slack.

G.W. Porter's Barrows   *by Dr. W. C. Rupture MD*
(The Hayloft Press   1/9)

There is rich variety in G W platform vehicles and each station seems to have its own traditions. I was surprised to read that the split-pins which secure the trolley wheels are inserted from right to left east of Bath while, to the west, it's the other way round. The author tells us that this is due to the Earth's spin and it is for the same reason that the left-hand trolley castors oscillate violently east of Bath and the right-hand ones going west. On the Birmingham line both castors oscillate for reasons science has yet to find a satisfactory explanation. A rather esoteric work.

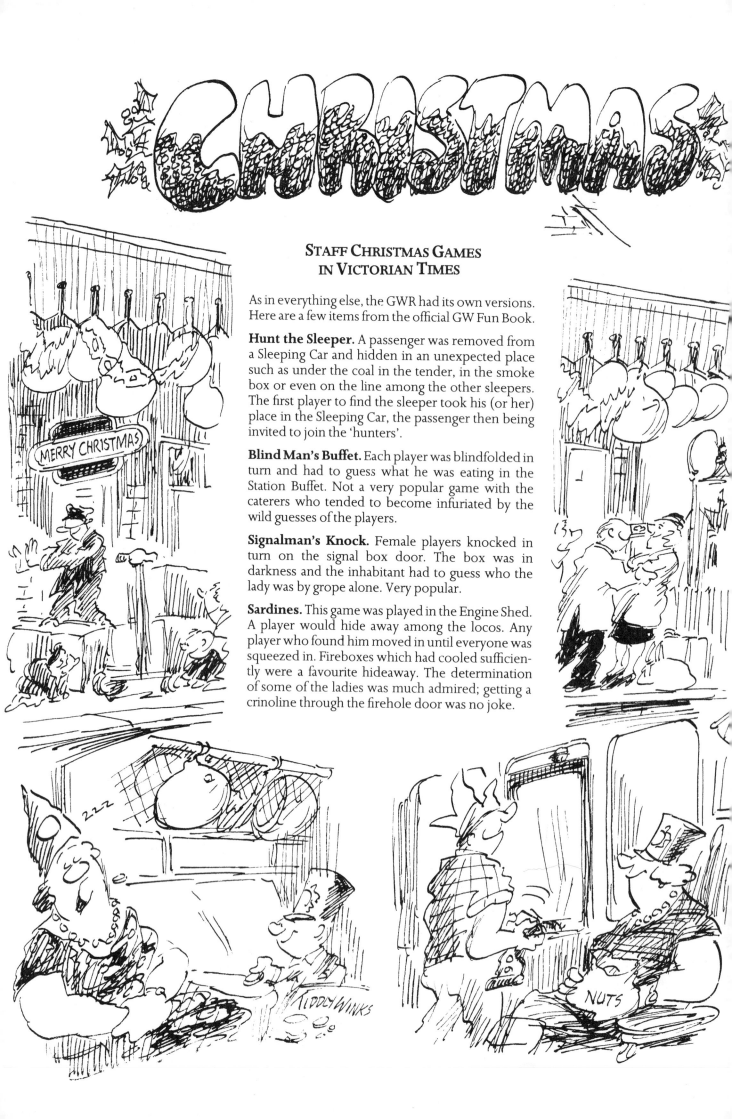

CHRISTMAS

STAFF CHRISTMAS GAMES IN VICTORIAN TIMES

As in everything else, the GWR had its own versions. Here are a few items from the official GW Fun Book.

Hunt the Sleeper. A passenger was removed from a Sleeping Car and hidden in an unexpected place such as under the coal in the tender, in the smoke box or even on the line among the other sleepers. The first player to find the sleeper took his (or her) place in the Sleeping Car, the passenger then being invited to join the 'hunters'.

Blind Man's Buffet. Each player was blindfolded in turn and had to guess what he was eating in the Station Buffet. Not a very popular game with the caterers who tended to become infuriated by the wild guesses of the players.

Signalman's Knock. Female players knocked in turn on the signal box door. The box was in darkness and the inhabitant had to guess who the lady was by grope alone. Very popular.

Sardines. This game was played in the Engine Shed. A player would hide away among the locos. Any player who found him moved in until everyone was squeezed in. Fireboxes which had cooled sufficiently were a favourite hideaway. The determination of some of the ladies was much admired; getting a crinoline through the firehole door was no joke.